Excel 2016
for Mac
Pivot Tables

TIM HILL

Questing Vole Press

Excel 2016 for Mac Pivot Tables
by Tim Hill

Editor: Kevin Debenjak
Proofreader: Janet Ott
Compositor: Kim Frees
Cover: Questing Vole Press

Contents

CHAPTER 1

Pivot Table Basics

You can use Excel's **pivot tables** to quickly create concise, flexible summaries of long lists of raw values, without having to write new formulas, copy and paste cells, or reorganize rows and columns. Pivot tables are **dynamic**: if you create a pivot table from, say, census data, then you can drag your mouse to rearrange the table so that it summarizes any variables of interest—age, gender, location, education, income, and so on. Rearranging a pivot table by swapping or moving rows and columns is called **pivoting**: turning the same information to view it at different angles. The jargon associated with pivot tables ("*n*-dimensional cross tabulations") makes them look complex, but they're really no more than an easy way to build flexible summary tables.

Excel offers other features for analyzing large amounts of data—including outlines, automatic subtotals, and statistical functions—but if you're working with hundreds (or hundreds of thousands) of rows, then pivot tables are the best way to look at the same information in different ways, summarize data on the fly, and spot trends and relationships.

Downloading the Sample Workbook

To create a pivot table, you need a long list of raw data values to summarize. (A short list works too but doesn't show the real power of pivot tables.) To follow along with the examples in this book, download the Excel workbook **orders16.xlsx** from *questingvolepress.com*. In orders16.xlsx, the worksheet named Source Data contains a list of 2155 records (rows) from grocery-item orders (Figure 1.1).

	A	B	C	D	E	F	G	H	I
1	Order ID	Product	Category	Unit Price	Quantity	Customer	Ship City	Ship Country	Order Date
2	10248	Singaporean Hokkien Fried Mee	Grains/Cereals	9.8	10	Vins et alcools Chevalier	Reims	France	04-Aug-94
3	10248	Mozzarella di Giovanni	Dairy Products	34.8	5	Vins et alcools Chevalier	Reims	France	04-Aug-94
4	10248	Queso Cabrales	Dairy Products	14	12	Vins et alcools Chevalier	Reims	France	04-Aug-94
5	10249	Tofu	Produce	18.6	9	Toms Spezialitäten	Münster	Germany	05-Aug-94
6	10249	Manjimup Dried Apples	Produce	42.4	40	Toms Spezialitäten	Münster	Germany	05-Aug-94
7	10250	Louisiana Fiery Hot Pepper Sauce	Condiments	16.8	15	Hanari Carnes	Rio de Janeiro	Brazil	08-Aug-94
8	10250	Jack's New England Clam Chowder	Seafood	7.7	10	Hanari Carnes	Rio de Janeiro	Brazil	08-Aug-94
9	10250	Manjimup Dried Apples	Produce	42.4	35	Hanari Carnes	Rio de Janeiro	Brazil	08-Aug-94
10	10251	Louisiana Fiery Hot Pepper Sauce	Condiments	16.8	20	Victuailles en stock	Lyon	France	08-Aug-94
11	10251	Gustaf's Knäckebröd	Grains/Cereals	16.8	6	Victuailles en stock	Lyon	France	08-Aug-94
12	10251	Ravioli Angelo	Grains/Cereals	15.6	15	Victuailles en stock	Lyon	France	08-Aug-94
13	10252	Sir Rodney's Marmalade	Confections	64.8	40	Suprêmes délices	Charleroi	Belgium	09-Aug-94
14	10252	Geitost	Dairy Products	2	25	Suprêmes délices	Charleroi	Belgium	09-Aug-94
15	10252	Camembert Pierrot	Dairy Products	27.2	40	Suprêmes délices	Charleroi	Belgium	09-Aug-94
16	10253	Maxilaku	Confections	16	40	Hanari Carnes	Rio de Janeiro	Brazil	10-Aug-94
17	10253	Chartreuse verte	Beverages	14.4	42	Hanari Carnes	Rio de Janeiro	Brazil	10-Aug-94
18	10253	Gorgonzola Telino	Dairy Products	10	20	Hanari Carnes	Rio de Janeiro	Brazil	10-Aug-94
19	10254	Pâté chinois	Meat/Poultry	19.2	21	Chop-suey Chinese	Bern	Switzerland	11-Aug-94
20	10254	Longlife Tofu	Produce	8	21	Chop-suey Chinese	Bern	Switzerland	11-Aug-94

Source Data +

Figure 1.1 The worksheet Source Data in the sample workbook contains the data used for the examples in this book.

Data Requirements for Pivot Tables

Pivot tables let you make comparisons and answer specific questions. To work well with pivot tables, a data list needs to meet the following criteria.

At least one column has duplicate values

Pivot tables are used to divide a list into logical **levels** (categories) and calculate statistics for each level. In the sample orders list, the column Customer, for example, has multiple records with the same value (denoting repeat customers). You can summarize the items ordered by each customer where each distinct customer is one level. In real-life data, the number of distinct values in a categorical column ranges from a few (gender or marital status, for example) to a few hundred (geographic location or part number); beyond a few hundred distinct values, analysis becomes unwieldy unless you group or filter categories.

At least one column has numerical values

Numerical values are used to calculate statistics (sum, count, average, maximum, percentage, custom formula, and more) for each column and level of interest. For non-numerical columns, the only statistics that you can calculate are frequency tabulations: counts of the number of levels (distinct values) in the column.

Sample Workbook Columns

The orders list in the sample workbook contains the columns listed in Table 1.1.

Table 1.1 Data columns in the sample workbook

Column	Data Type	Description
Order ID	Categorical	Identifies an order uniquely. An order for multiple products spans multiple rows. Order 10248, for example, spans rows 2, 3, and 4 (one product per row). Though the order IDs are numbers (10248, 10249,...), this column is actually categorical because it makes no sense to do mathematical operations on its values (summing IDs is meaningless, for example).
Product	Categorical	The brand name of the ordered product (Jack's New England Clam Chowder, Manjimup Dried Apples, and so on).
Category	Categorical	The type of the ordered product (Seafood, Produce, and so on).
Unit Price	Numerical	The selling price of a single unit of the ordered product.
Quantity	Numerical	The number of units of the product sold in the order.
Customer	Categorical	The name of the buyer.
Ship City	Categorical	The city (in Ship Country) where the order was shipped.
Ship Country	Categorical	The country where the order was shipped.
Order Date	Categorical	The date that the order was placed.

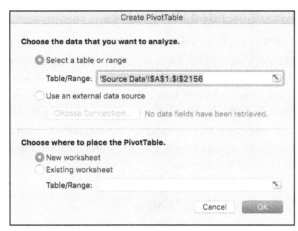

Figure 1.2 In the Create PivotTable dialog box, specify the pivot table's source data and its destination worksheet.

Creating Pivot Tables

To create a new pivot table, you run the Create Pivot-Table wizard, which lets you select the data to summarize and position the pivot table on a worksheet. You can then structure the pivot table and organize and filter your data however you like.

To create a pivot table:

1   Select the range of cells (including column titles) that you want to use for the pivot table. Alternatively, select a single cell in the range and Excel will expand the range automatically; if Excel misidentifies the range, you can fix it in the next step.

It's actually preferable to use a *table* (Insert tab > Tables group > Table, or press Ctrl+T) instead of selecting a range of cells. That way, Excel automatically accounts for any new rows that you add to the source data when you refresh the pivot table (page 14). If you use a range instead of a table, then you must redefine the pivot table's data source if you add new rows to the end of the range (PivotTable Analyze tab > Data group > Change Data Source).

2   Choose Insert tab > Tables group > PivotTable.

Alternatively, if you're creating a pivot table for a table that you defined with Insert tab > Tables group > Table, you can select any cell in the table and then choose Table tab > Summarize with PivotTable.

The Create PivotTable dialog box opens (Figure 1.2). Excel automatically chooses "Select a table or range", with the table name or cell range that you selected. (To create a pivot table based on an external database, you must first configure your database as an external data source: choose Data tab > Get External Data.)

continues on next page

3 Select "New worksheet" to create a new worksheet for the pivot table (typically the best option).

Alternatively, choose "Existing worksheet" to insert the pivot table on a worksheet that's already in your workbook. Specify the cell reference for the top-left corner of the pivot table. Excel overwrites any values in the target cells when it creates the pivot table.

In general, it's safest to place a pivot table on its own new worksheet. If you restructure the pivot table, it can grow to overwrite other values on the sheet (Excel warns you before overwriting existing data).

4 Click OK.

Excel inserts the new pivot table (Figure 1.3). The pivot table appears as an empty placeholder until you define the rows, columns, and values to use to summarize the source data. When you select a cell inside the pivot table, Excel displays the PivotTable Builder on the right, which lists all the columns in the source data.

If you chose to create a new worksheet, Excel gives the sheet a generic name (Sheet1 or whatever) and then places it before the worksheet that contains the source data. You can rename the new worksheet (double-click its worksheet tab) or drag its worksheet tab left or right to reposition it.

Recommended Pivot Tables

The Recommended PivotTables feature lets you create a new pivot table quickly based on Excel's analysis of your data. Select the source data and then choose Insert tab > Tables group > Recommended PivotTables. Excel displays the recommended pivot table based on the data. If you don't like Excel's suggestion, use the PivotTable Builder to change the layout.

Deleting a Pivot Table

A pivot table is a monolithic grid, meaning deletion is all-or-nothing. Excel won't let you insert or delete individual cells, rows, or columns in a pivot table.

To delete a pivot table:

- Select any cell in the pivot table and then choose PivotTable Analyze tab > Actions group > Clear > Clear All.

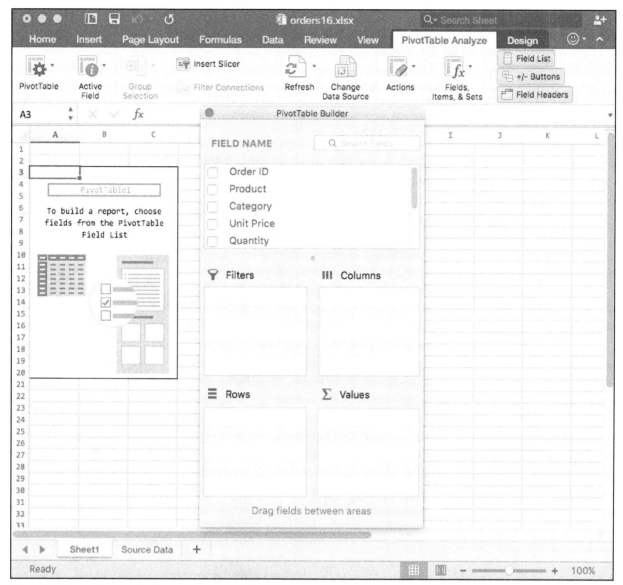

Figure 1.3 A newly created pivot table on a new worksheet.

Laying Out Pivot Tables

To lay out a pivot table, you use the **PivotTable Build-er** (Figure 1.4). Drag columns, called **fields**, from the field list into any of the four boxes underneath (use the search box to find fields quickly in long lists). You can also select the checkbox next to a field; Excel will place it in a box depending on the field's data type (if Excel guesses wrong, drag the field to the correct box). Excel updates the pivot table dynamically as you add, rearrange, or remove fields in the four lower boxes.

The PivotTable Builder appears when you select any cell in a pivot table. If it doesn't appear, choose PivotTable Analyze tab > Field List.

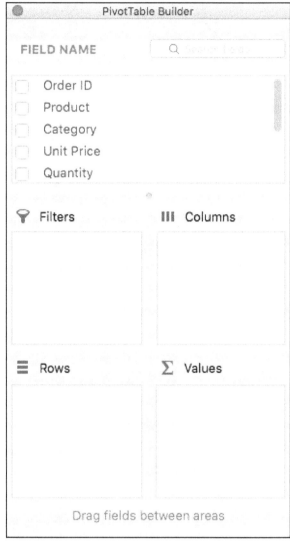

Figure 1.4 Use the PivotTable Builder to lay out your pivot table and rearrange fields.

Row or Column Label?

Choosing whether a field appears as a row or column label is a matter of formatting and readability (either way, the same data are displayed). Fields with long category names or many distinct values typically work better as row labels (as column labels, they stretch or proliferate columns). The Product field, for example, works best as a row label; as a column label, the pivot table would be 77 columns wide (Alice Mutton, Aniseed Syrup,..., Zaanse koeken) and hard to read and print.

A pivot table has four areas:

Values

These fields are the numerical values for which you want to display sums, averages, counts, and other statistics. You can drag the Unit Price field here, for example, to calculate price statistics. (If you drag a non-numerical field to Values, only counts are calculated.) For details, see Chapter 4.

Rows

These fields group the data into levels, one level per row. You can drag the Category field here, for example, to show product categories (Beverages, Condiments, and so on).

Columns

These fields also create levels, one level per column. You can use both Rows and Columns to divide your data in multiple ways in the same pivot table. Drag Ship Country to Rows, Category to Columns, and Quantity to Values, for example. The pivot table divides sales figures into rows by country and columns by product category, answering the question, "Which types of products sell best in each country?".

Filters

These fields limit the data displayed in the pivot table. To show a breakdown of U.S.-only sales by product category, for example, drag Ship Country to Filters and then configure the filter to show only "USA" values. For details, see "Report Filters" on page 44.

Rearranging (Pivoting) a Pivot Table

In the PivotTable Builder, you can remove or move fields at any time to rearrange (pivot) the pivot table.

To remove a field from a pivot table:

- Do any of the following:

  ▶ Drag the field from any box out of the Pivot-Table Builder (the mouse pointer changes to a circle-slash symbol as you drag).

  ▶ Click the field's Info button (labeled *i*) in a box and then click Hide in the PivotTable Field dialog box that opens.

  ▶ Clear the checkbox next to the field name in the field list.

To move a field from one area to another:

- Drag the field from one box to another.

Moving a Pivot Table

You can move a pivot table to a new worksheet or an existing one. Select any cell in the pivot table and then choose PivotTable Analyze tab > Actions group > Move PivotTable.

PivotTable Options

You can change the most common pivot-table settings by using the ribbon or the PivotTable Builder, but you can find many others in the PivotTable Options dialog box (Figure 1.5). To open it, right-click any cell in the pivot table and then choose PivotTable Options (or choose PivotTable Analyze tab > PivotTable group > Options).

Tip: Settings changed in the PivotTable Options dialog box apply to only the active pivot table.

Figure 1.5 Use the PivotTable Options dialog box to fine-tune the selected pivot table.

Layout Examples

The following example creates a summary that compares products and shipping locations. The result is a **two-dimensional** pivot table. Most pivot tables seen in practice are two-dimensional, meaning that they summarize two different fields.

Tip: If you're using the sample workbook to follow along, the look of your pivot tables depends on which report layout (compact, outline, or tabular form) you choose (page 15).

To compare products and shipping locations:

1 If necessary, create a new pivot table (page 5).

2 In the PivotTable Builder, drag the Product field to the Rows box underneath.

   Excel fills in all the product names from the source data from top to bottom (in alphabetical order), one product per row.

3 Drag the Ship Country field to the Columns box.

   Excel fills in all the country names from the source data from left to right (in alphabetical order), one country per column.

4 Drag the Quantity field to the Values box.

   This step chooses which data to examine. Excel fills the pivot table with the numbers of products that were ordered by customers in various countries (Figure 1.6). The default calculation for pivot tables is the sum of each field in the Values box (note the label "Sum of Quantity" in the Values box). In this example, each value is the total number of units of a specific product shipped to a specific country.

   Pivot tables also calculate subtotals and grand totals. To see them, scroll to rightmost or bottommost end of the pivot table. The grand total is in the bottom-right corner.

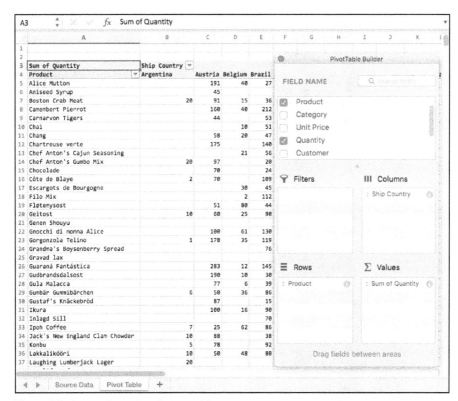

Figure 1.6 A two-dimensional pivot table.

You can also *nest* fields by placing them together in the Rows or Columns box. For example, starting with an empty pivot table, drag Product to the Rows box, drag Ship Country to the same box (placing it below Product), and then drag Quantity to the Values box (Figure 1.7). The order of fields within a box determines their nesting order in the pivot table (here, Ship Country is nested within Product). For details, see Chapter 2.

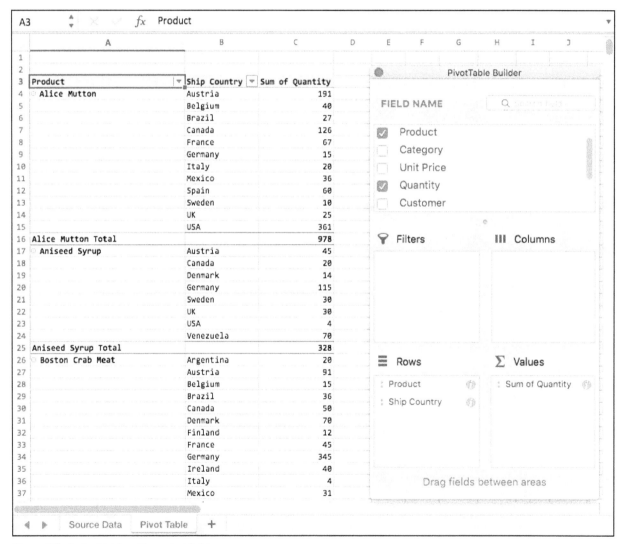

Figure 1.7 A pivot table with nested fields.

A **one-dimensional** pivot table has a single field in either the Columns or Rows box (but not both). For example, starting with an empty pivot table, drag Product to the Rows box and then drag Quantity to the Values box (Figure 1.8). The resulting pivot table simply totals the number of units sold by product.

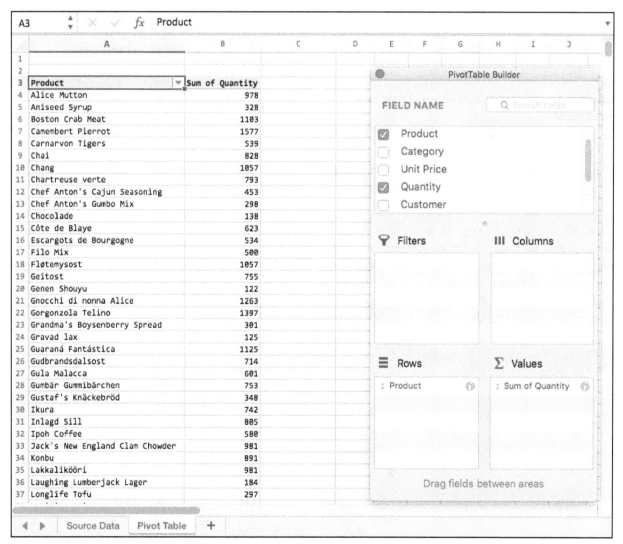

Figure 1.8 A one-dimensional pivot table.

Refreshing Pivot Tables

Unlike formulas, charts, and most other elements in Excel, pivot tables don't auto-update when the underlying data change. If you change the source data, the pivot table can show out-of-date calculations. A **refresh** makes Excel scan the source data and recalculate the pivot table.

To refresh a pivot table manually:

- Do any of the following:

  ▸ Right-click the pivot table and then choose Refresh Data.

  ▸ Select any cell in the pivot table and then choose PivotTable Analyze tab > Data group > Refresh arrow > Refresh (Figure 1.9), or click Refresh All to refresh all pivot tables in the workbook.

To autorefresh a pivot table when you open a workbook:

- Select any cell in the pivot table and then choose PivotTable Analyze tab > PivotTable group > Options > Data pane > select "Refresh data when opening file".

Tip: A refresh can take a long time depending on the amount of source data, the complexity of the pivot table, the speed of your computer, and other factors. After starting a refresh, you can review its status or cancel it at any time by choosing Refresh Status or Cancel Refresh from the Refresh menu.

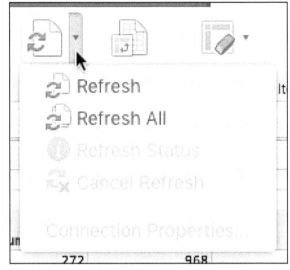

Figure 1.9 Click the arrow on the Refresh button to choose an option for recalculating a pivot table.

Autoformatting on Refresh

If a pivot table becomes misformatted when you refresh it, select the "AutoFit column widths on update" and "Preserve cell formatting on update" checkboxes on the Layout pane in the PivotTable Options dialog box (PivotTable Analyze tab > PivotTable group > Options).

Formatting Pivot Tables

When you select a cell in a pivot table, the ribbon sprouts two contextual tabs: PivotTable Analyze and Design. These tabs are similar to the ones that appear when you select a chart, table, or picture.

The PivotTable Analyze tab accesses advanced features like grouping, custom calculations, and filtering (all covered in later chapters). The Design tab (Figure 1.10) changes the appearance of the active pivot table.

The Design tab has three groups:

Layout

Choose a preset option that controls spacing and subtotals.

Subtotals. Show subtotals at the top or bottom of each level. This setting applies only if fields are nested; that is, the Rows or Columns box contains more than one field (Chapter 2).

Grand Totals. Show or hide the grand totals at the end of each row or column.

Report Layout. By default, pivot tables are shown in **compact form**: all row labels are merged into a single column, and each column just wide enough to fit that column's widest entry. In **outline form**, each row label gets its own column, and each column is as wide as the widest column in the whole pivot table (which occupies much more space). **Tabular form** is like outline form but shows subtotals (extra rows) at

the bottom of each level or group. You can also **repeat labels** to show values of nested fields in all row and column labels. In compact form, you can control how far row levels are indented: choose PivotTable Analyze tab > PivotTable group > Options > Layout pane > "Indent row labels when in compact form".

Blank Rows. Show or hide blank lines between levels or groups. This option applies only if the Rows box has more than one field.

Tip: If you're going to copy or export a pivot table from Excel to another program (such as a database or accounting program), use outline form and repeating labels.

PivotTables Style Options

If you don't want to apply the style formatting to headers, clear Row Headers or Column Headers. If you don't want shading to alternate from one row or column to the next, clear Banded Rows or Banded Columns. (To show or hide field headers for rows and columns, choose PivotTable Analyze tab > Field Headers.)

PivotTables Styles

Click a style to change the colors and shading of the pivot table (to create a custom style, click "New PivotTable Style"). The colors come from the workbook theme that you're using. To use different colors, choose Page Layout tab > Themes group > Themes.

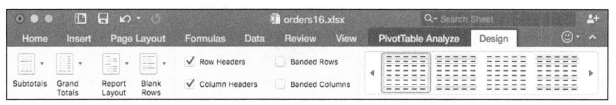

Figure 1.10 Use the Design tab to format the active pivot table.

Showing a Value's Source Data

If you spot a trend, unexpected relationship, or an outlier (suspicious observation) in a pivot table, you can "drill down" to see exactly how the value was calculated. To do so, double-click any value cell in a pivot table. Excel creates a new worksheet containing copies of only the records that were used to calculate that cell's value. This method is superior to the tedious alternative: switching to the worksheet that contains the original source data and then searching for the corresponding records.

The pivot table in Figure 1.11 shows how product categories (rows) perform in each country (columns). Double-click cell B5, for example, and Excel adds a worksheet containing copies of the seven records (in a formatted table) whose Quantity values were summed to produce Argentine beverage sales (Figure 1.12).

After you finish examining the data, you can delete the worksheet that contains the copied records (right-click the worksheet tab at the bottom of the window and then choose Delete). The original source data aren't touched when you delete the copy.

If you spot an error in the copied records, you must flip to the original source data to fix it. Obvious, yes, but it's easy to absentmindedly change the *copied* records and then wonder why the refreshed pivot table doesn't change.

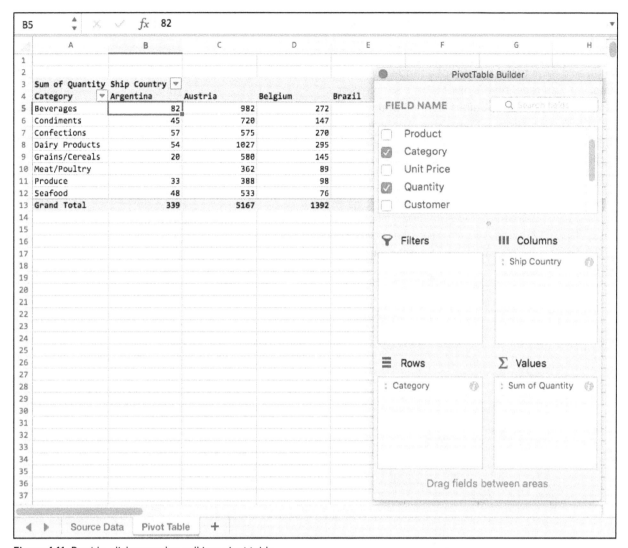

Figure 1.11 Double-click any value cell in a pivot table...

	A	B	C	D	E	F	G	H	I	J
A1			*fx*	Order ID						
1	Order ID	Product	Category	Unit Price	Quantity	Customer	Ship City	Ship Country	Order Date	
2	11054	Laughing L	Beverages	14	20	Cactus Comi	Buenos Aires	Argentina	5/28/96	
3	10986	Lakkalikööl	Beverages	18	10	Océano Atlá	Buenos Aires	Argentina	4/29/96	
4	10937	Sasquatch	Beverages	14	20	Cactus Comi	Buenos Aires	Argentina	4/9/96	
5	10828	Côte de Bl	Beverages	263.5	2	Rancho gran	Buenos Aires	Argentina	2/13/96	
6	10819	Rhönbräu K	Beverages	7.75	20	Cactus Comi	Buenos Aires	Argentina	2/7/96	
7	10819	Ipoh Coffe	Beverages	46	7	Cactus Comi	Buenos Aires	Argentina	2/7/96	
8	10521	Steeleye S	Beverages	18	3	Cactus Comi	Buenos Aires	Argentina	5/30/95	

Figure 1.12 ...to see copies of the source records that were used to calculate that value.

Changing a Pivot Table's Source Data

If you add rows to the bottom of a range of source data, you can redefine the pivot table's source data to include those rows. Select any cell in the pivot table and then choose PivotTable Analyze tab > Data group > Change Source Data. The same fix applies if you add columns to the right edge of the source data.

Tip: If the source data are in an Excel table (Insert tab > Tables group > Table), then you don't have to change the range—newly added rows are displayed automatically when you refresh the pivot table (page 14).

CHAPTER 2

Nesting Fields

You saw examples of one- and two-dimensional pivot tables in the preceding chapter, but Excel doesn't limit the number of fields in a pivot table.

Adding Nested Fields

Each time that you add a new field, Excel subdivides, or **nests**, the current fields.

To add additional (nested) fields to a pivot table:

1   Select any cell in the pivot table.

    Excel shows the PivotTable Builder.

2   In the PivotTable Builder, drag fields from the field list to the Rows or Columns boxes underneath.

    The order of fields within a box determines their nesting order in the pivot table.

Consider a pivot table with the settings (Figure 2.1):

Rows: Product, Ship Country
Columns: (empty)
Values: Quantity (summarized by Sum)
Filters: (empty)

Each row in this pivot table shows the total units of a specific product shipped to a specific country.

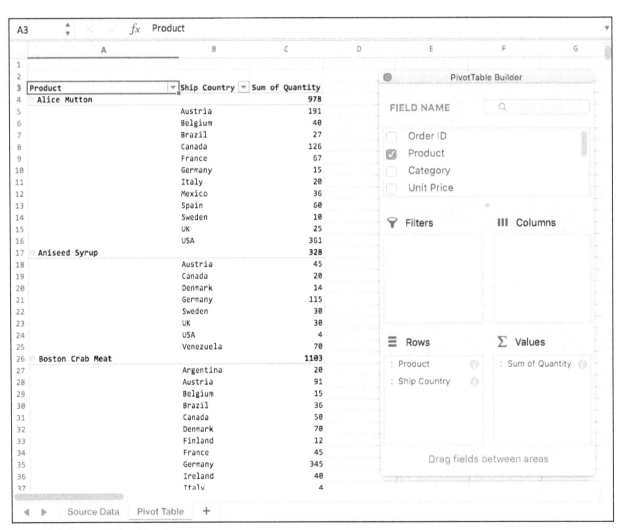

Figure 2.1 A pivot table with subgroups.

Excessive nesting can make a pivot table uninformative or unwieldy. If the number of rows in a pivot table is close to the number of rows in the underlying source data, then that pivot table isn't truly a summary. Another sign of an overnested pivot table is an excessive number of empty cells (wasted space). Consider a pivot table with the settings (Figure 2.2):

Rows: Category, Order Date
Columns: Ship Country
Values: Quantity (summarized by Sum)
Filters: (empty)

The rows in this pivot table are grouped by category and subdivided by order date. At 1605 rows (not counting subtotals or blank values), this pivot table isn't much smaller than the source data (2155 rows). The problem is that few orders fall on the same date. And when they do, they're usually for different product categories. Consequently, many rows show results for only a single order, rather than true totals. This pivot table is **sparse** (contains many empty cells) because each row is further broken up into columns by country.

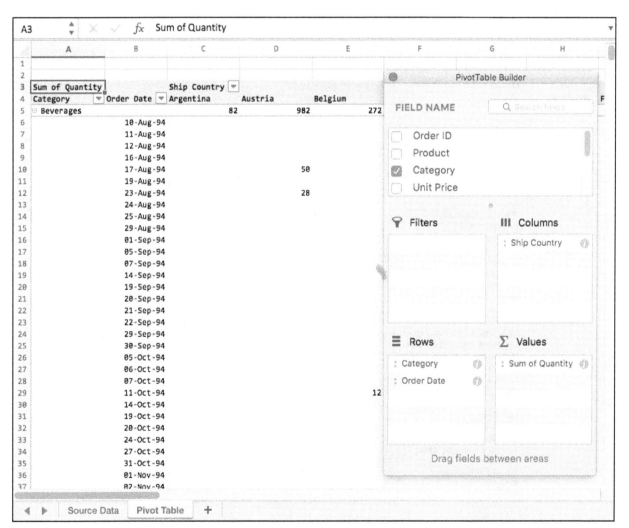

Figure 2.2 A pivot table with excessive nesting.

Nesting works best for closely related fields, such as Category and Product (each product falls in one category) (Figure 2.3).

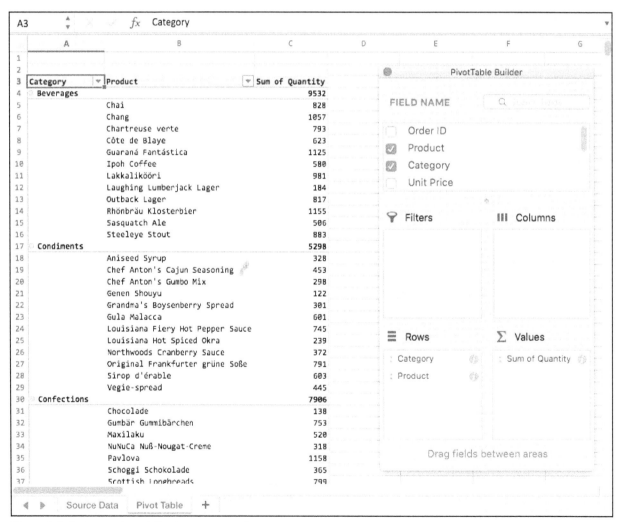

Figure 2.3 A pivot table with Product nested in Category.

Or Ship Country and Ship City (each city is located in one country) (Figure 2.4).

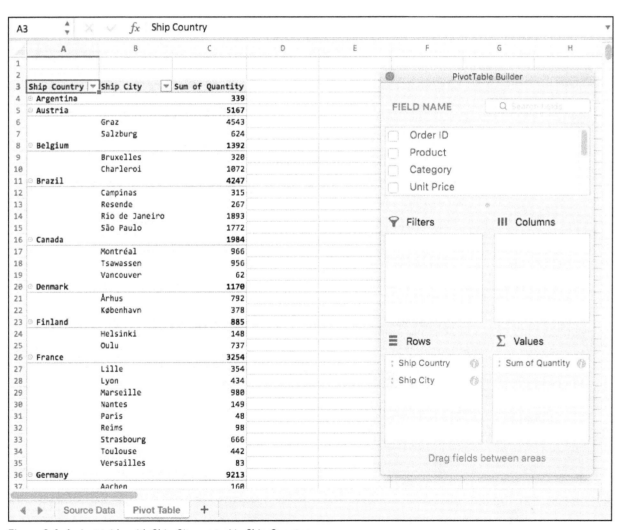

Figure 2.4 A pivot table with Ship City nested in Ship Country.

Make sure that you place the fields in the correct order in the Rows or Columns box; otherwise, you'll get silly results. Consider a pivot table with the settings (Figure 2.5):

Rows: Product, Category
Columns: (empty)
Values: Quantity (summarized by Sum)
Filters: (empty)

This pivot table groups the records by product and then subdivides the products by category, resulting in an unhelpful pivot table where each group

contains a single subgroup (because each product falls in only one category). To fix this pivot table, swap the row labels (that is, drag Product below Category in the Rows box).

To reorder fields in a pivot table:

1   Select any cell in the pivot table.

    Excel shows the PivotTable Builder.

2   In the PivotTable Builder, drag fields up or down within a box.

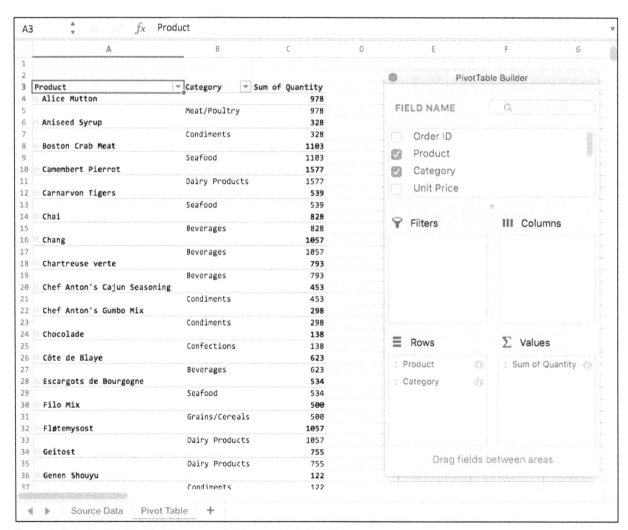

Figure 2.5 A pivot table with Category nested incorrectly in Product.

Showing and Hiding Levels

You can show (**expand**) or hide (**collapse**) individual levels in nested rows or columns, concealing the parts of a pivot table that you don't want to see. In a pivot table that nests Product within Category, for example, you can show only the products in a specific category and hide the rest (Figure 2.6).

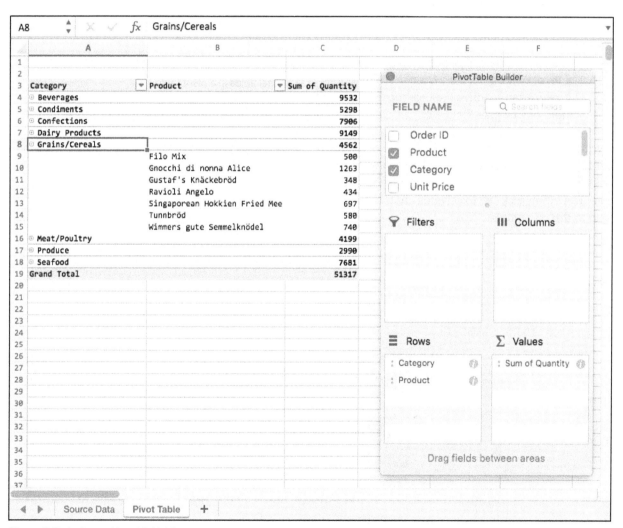

Figure 2.6 A pivot table with hidden groups.

To show or hide specific levels:

- Do any of the following:

  ▶ Click the plus (+) or minus (–) button next to the level name in the pivot table (click again to toggle visibility). If the +/– buttons aren't visible, choose PivotTable Analyze tab > +/– Buttons.

  ▶ Double-click the cell containing the level name (double-click again to toggle visibility).

To show or hide all levels:

- Do any of the following:

  ▶ In the target field, right-click any cell containing a level name and then choose Show Detail or Hide Detail from the Group and Outline submenu.

  ▶ In the target field, select any cell containing a level name and then choose PivotTable Analyze tab > Active Field group > Expand Field or Collapse Field.

If you try to expand an innermost nested level, Excel opens the Show Detail dialog box listing all the fields *not* currently showing (Figure 2.7). If you select a field and then click OK, Excel adds another nested field to the pivot table.

Figure 2.7 Use the Show Detail dialog box to nest additional fields in a pivot table.

CHAPTER 3

Grouping Items

Pivot tables let you combine items into **groups**, which you can use to subset related values that can't be easily combined by sorting, filtering, or other means. Numbers, dates, times, and user-selected items can be grouped.

Grouping by Selected Items

To create a custom group, select the items in the pivot table that you want to group, either by clicking or dragging, and then choose PivotTable Analyze tab > Group Selection group > Group Selection (or right-click a selected cell and then choose Group and Outline > Group from the shortcut menu).

Tip: To select adjacent cells, click the first cell and then Shift-click the last cell. To select nonadjacent cells, Command-click each cell.

Consider a pivot table with the settings:

Rows: Ship Country
Columns: (empty)
Values: Quantity (summarized by Sum)
Filters: (empty)

In the pivot table, Command-click Canada, Mexico, and USA; right-click any selected item; and then choose Group and Outline > Group (Figure 3.1).

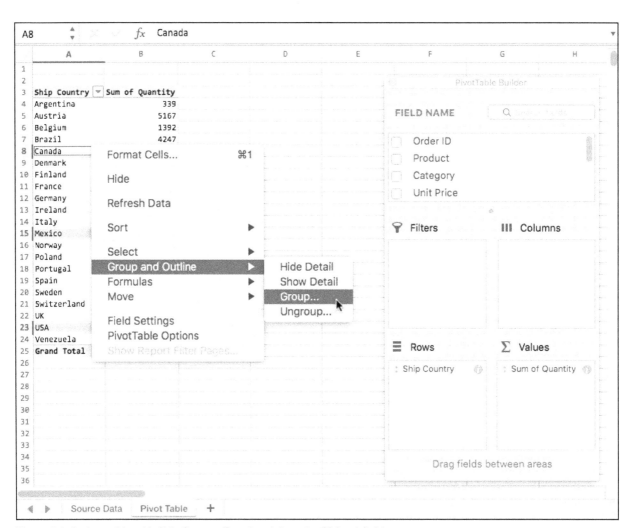

Figure 3.1 A pivot table with Ship Country (Rows) and Quantity (Values) fields.

Replace the default group name (Group1) with a meaningful name (North America) (Figure 3.2). Excel also creates a new virtual field named Ship Country2 in the Rows box, which you can pivot on (drag Ship Country2 to the Columns box, for example). To remove the grouping, right-click the group name and then choose Group and Outline > Ungroup.

Nested Groups

You can create any number of groups and even create nested groups (groups of groups) (Figure 3.3). When you create nested groups, it's usually easiest to define the broadest (outermost) group first and then progress to the innermost groups.

A8 | fx North America

	A	B	C
1			
2			
3	Row Labels	Sum of Quantity	
4	Argentina	339	
5	Austria	5167	
6	Belgium	1392	
7	Brazil	4247	
8	North America		
9	Canada	1984	
10	Mexico	1025	
11	USA	9330	
12	Denmark	1170	
13	Finland	885	
14	France	3254	
15	Germany	9213	
16	Ireland	1684	
17	Italy	822	
18	Norway	161	
19	Poland	205	
20	Portugal	533	
21	Spain	718	
22	Sweden	2235	
23	Switzerland	1275	
24	UK	2742	
25	Venezuela	2936	
26	Grand Total	51317	

Figure 3.2 A pivot table with a Ship Country group.

A3 | fx Row Labels

	A	B
1		
2		
3	Row Labels	Sum of Quantity
4	World	
5	Americas	
6	South America	
7	Argentina	339
8	Brazil	4247
9	Venezuela	2936
10	North America	
11	Canada	1984
12	Mexico	1025
13	USA	9330
14	Europe	
15	Austria	5167
16	Belgium	1392
17	Denmark	1170
18	Finland	885
19	France	3254
20	Germany	9213
21	Ireland	1684
22	Italy	822
23	Norway	161
24	Poland	205
25	Portugal	533
26	Spain	718
27	Sweden	2235
28	Switzerland	1275
29	UK	2742
30	Grand Total	51317

Figure 3.3 A pivot table with nested Ship Country groups.

Grouping by Time Periods

When a field contains dates or times, you can create groups that summarize data by time periods (hours, months, years, and so on). You can use the Order Date field, for example, to summarize sales by month. Consider a pivot table with the settings (Figure 3.4):

Rows: Order Date
Columns: (empty)
Values: Quantity (summarized by Sum)
Filters: (empty)

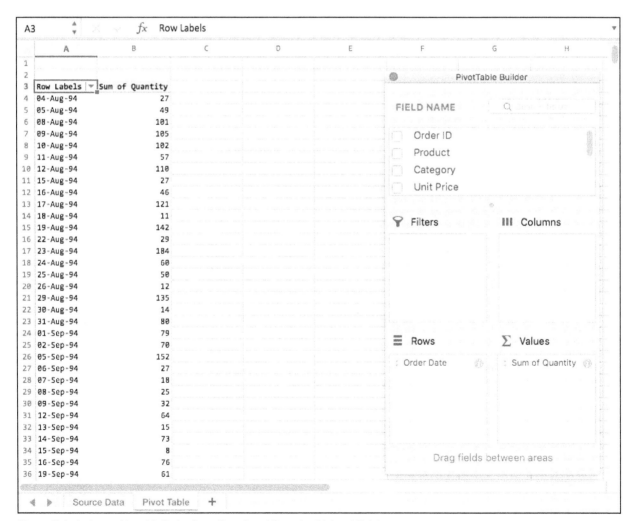

Figure 3.4 A pivot table with Order Date (Rows) and Quantity (Values) fields.

In the pivot table, right-click any cell in the Order Date (Rows) column and then select Group and Outline > Group from the shortcut menu. The Grouping dialog box opens (Figure 3.5). In the By list, select Months and Years (Command-click each list item to select or deselect it). Verify that the starting and ending dates are correct and then click OK.

The Order Date items in the pivot table are grouped by years and by months (Figure 3.6). Excel also creates a new virtual field named Years in the Rows box, which you can pivot on (drag Years to the Columns box, for example). To remove the grouping, right-click any cell in the Order Date (Rows) column and then choose Group and Outline > Ungroup.

Tip: If you select only Months (and not Years) in the By list, then months in different years are combined. The Aug item, for example, would show the combined quantities for 1994 *and* 1995 (the data stop in June, 1996).

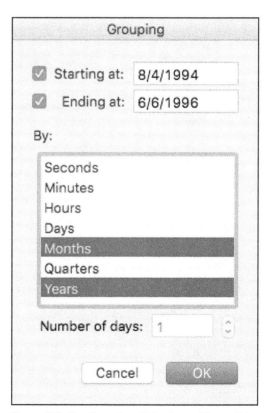

Figure 3.5 The Grouping dialog box with monthly and yearly groupings specified.

	A	B	C
	A3	fx	Row Labels
1			
2			
3	Row Labels ▼	Sum of Quantity	
4	1994		
5	Aug	1462	
6	Sep	1322	
7	Oct	1124	
8	Nov	1669	
9	Dec	1804	
10	1995		
11	Jan	2200	
12	Feb	1951	
13	Mar	2582	
14	Apr	1622	
15	May	2060	
16	Jun	2164	
17	Jul	1635	
18	Aug	2054	
19	Sep	1861	
20	Oct	2343	
21	Nov	2657	
22	Dec	1878	
23	1996		
24	Jan	2682	
25	Feb	3293	
26	Mar	3288	
27	Apr	4065	
28	May	4957	
29	Jun	644	
30	Grand Total	51317	

Figure 3.6 A pivot table grouped by month and year.

Grouping by Weeks

You can also group by week (or any fixed span of days). In the Grouping dialog box (Figure 3.7), select only Days (nothing else) in the By list and then type 7 in the "Number of days" box. Clear the "Starting at" checkbox and then adjust the start date to fall on the first day (typically, Sunday or Monday) of the first week of interest. If you like, adjust the end date too. Click OK.

Each row in the resulting pivot table shows the start and end dates of each week (Figure 3.8).

Figure 3.7 The Grouping dialog box with weekly (7-day) groupings specified.

A3		✕	✓	fx	Row Labels

	A	B
1		
2		
3	Row Labels ▼	Sum of Quantity
4	8/1/94 - 8/7/94	76
5	8/8/94 - 8/14/94	475
6	8/15/94 - 8/21/94	347
7	8/22/94 - 8/28/94	335
8	8/29/94 - 9/4/94	378
9	9/5/94 - 9/11/94	254
10	9/12/94 - 9/18/94	236
11	9/19/94 - 9/25/94	410
12	9/26/94 - 10/2/94	273
13	10/3/94 - 10/9/94	301
14	10/10/94 - 10/16/94	367
15	10/17/94 - 10/23/94	147
16	10/24/94 - 10/30/94	289
17	10/31/94 - 11/6/94	158
18	11/7/94 - 11/13/94	555
19	11/14/94 - 11/20/94	325
20	11/21/94 - 11/27/94	294
21	11/28/94 - 12/4/94	531
22	12/5/94 - 12/11/94	349
23	12/12/94 - 12/18/94	311
24	12/19/94 - 12/25/94	609
25	12/26/94 - 1/1/95	361
26	1/2/95 - 1/8/95	473
27	1/9/95 - 1/15/95	385
28	1/16/95 - 1/22/95	365
29	1/23/95 - 1/29/95	688
30	1/30/95 - 2/5/95	859

Figure 3.8 A pivot table grouped by week.

Grouping by Numbers

You can group by numbers to create a **frequency distribution,** where each entry in the pivot table contains the frequency (count) of the occurrences of values within a particular group or interval. Consider a pivot table with the settings:

Rows: Quantity
Columns: (empty)
Values: Quantity (summarized by Sum)
Filters: (empty)

The pivot table shows the quantity of units sold and the corresponding number of orders. The goal is to determine how many quantities are in each 10-point range (1–10, 11–20, and so on).

In the pivot table, right-click any cell in the Quantity (Rows) column and then select Group and Outline > Group from the shortcut menu (Figure 3.9).

The Grouping dialog box opens (Figure 3.10). In the By box, type the size of the interval for each group (here, 10). Verify that the starting and ending points are correct and then click OK.

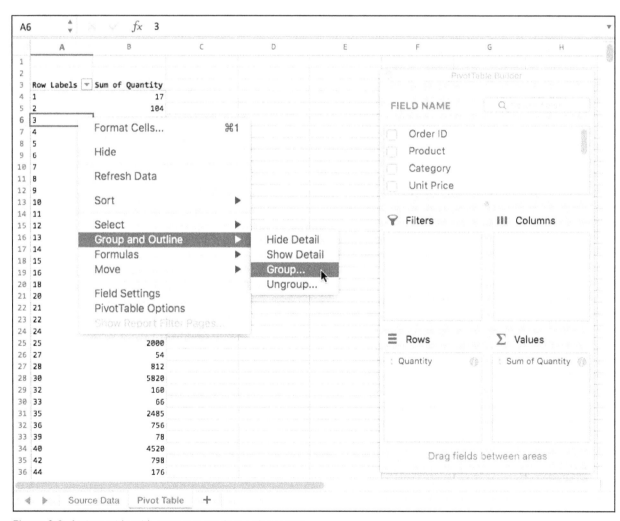

Figure 3.9 A pivot table with customer product-order counts.

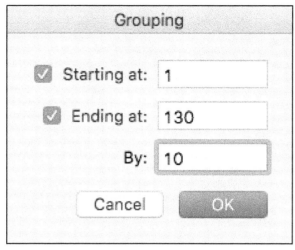

Figure 3.10 The Grouping dialog box with numeric interval groupings specified.

The Quantity items in the pivot table (Figure 3.11) are grouped in uniform intervals (bins). The groups start at 1 and end at 130, in increments of 10. A column chart of a frequency distribution is a histogram. To remove the grouping, right-click any cell in the Quantity (Rows) column and then choose Group and Outline > Ungroup.

Tip: By default, pivot tables don't display items with a count of zero. To make sure that your frequency distribution has no gaps between intervals, select any cell in the interval column, choose PivotTable Analyze tab > Active Field group > Field Settings, and then select "Show items with no data".

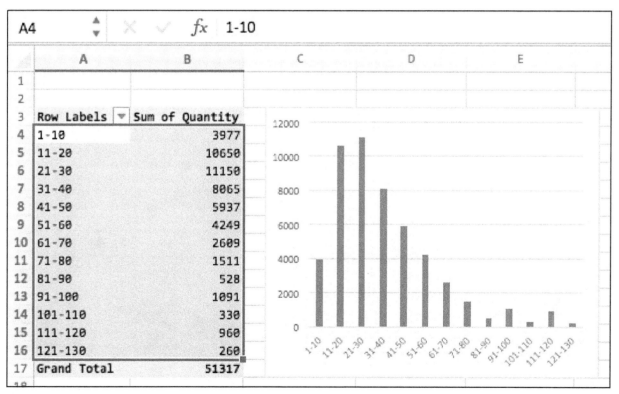

Figure 3.11 A pivot table grouped by numeric intervals, with a column chart (histogram).

CHAPTER 4

Calculations and Custom Formulas

When you add a field to the Values box in the PivotTable Builder, Excel (in most cases) sums all the values in that field, but you can also calculate common statistics, do multiple calculations in the same pivot table, and create custom formulas.

Calculating Common Statistics

Excel's preset calculations include common statistics: sum, count, average, maximum, percentage, and so on.

To choose a preset calculation:

1 Select any cell in the pivot table.

   Excel shows the PivotTable Builder.

2 In the PivotTable Builder, click the Info button (labeled *i*) in the target field ("Sum of Quantity", for example) in the Values box. Alternatively, select any cell in the target field in the pivot table and then choose PivotTable Analyze tab > Active Field group > Field Settings.

   The PivotTable Field dialog box opens.

3 In the "Summarize by" tab (Figure 4.1), choose a calculation in the list (Sum, Count, Average,...).

   Alternatively, click the "Show data as" tab (Figure 4.2) to choose a more-complex calculation (difference, percentage, running total, or index).

   You can also change the default field name by typing a new name in the Field Name box.

4 To format the field's values, click the Number button, choose or define a new format, and then click OK.

   You can change the number of decimal places, add a currency symbol, and so on.

5 Click OK to close the PivotTable Field dialog box.

   Excel refreshes the pivot table with the new calculations.

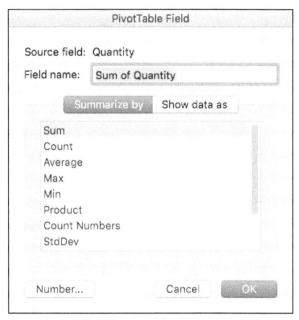

Figure 4.1 Use the Summarize By tab to choose a simple calculation or...

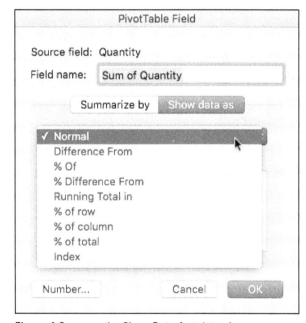

Figure 4.2 ...use the Show Data As tab to choose a more-complex calculation.

Specifying Values for Empty Cells

To specify what values appear in the empty cells in a pivot table (typically, a zero, a blank, or a text indicator such as *Missing*), right-click any cell in the pivot table and then choose Pivot-Table Options (or choose PivotTable Analyze tab > PivotTable group > Options). On the Display pane, enter the desired settings for the "Empty cells as" options.

Calculating Multiple Statistics

When you add multiple fields to the Values box, each field is calculated and shown in a separate column in the pivot table. To sum the Quantity and average the Unit Price, for example, drag both fields into the Values box and then follow the steps above to configure each field separately (Figure 4.3).

Similarly, you can do multiple calculations on the *same* field. To sum and average Quantity, for example, drag Quantity into the Values box twice and then configure the two Quantity fields separately.

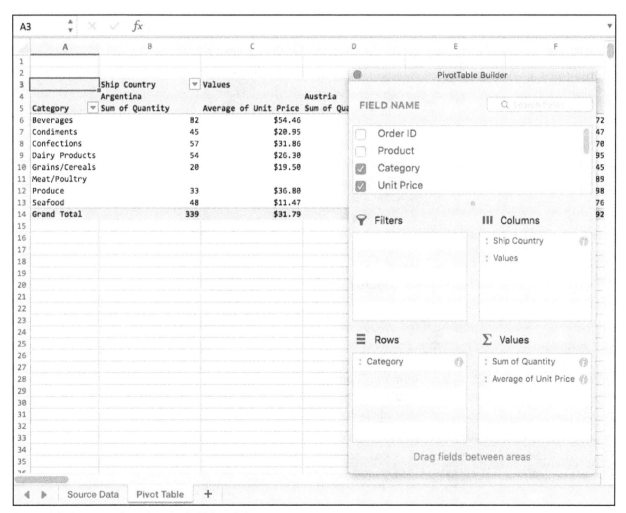

Figure 4.3 A pivot table with multiple Values fields.

Adding Custom Calculations

In addition to choosing a preset calculation, you can define a custom **calculated field** in a pivot table.

To add a calculated field:

1 Select any cell in the pivot table.

2 Choose PivotTable Analyze tab > Fields, Items, & Sets group > Calculated Field. Alternatively, right-click any cell in the pivot table and then choose Formulas > Calculated Field from the shortcut menu.

   The Insert Calculated Field dialog box opens (Figure 4.4).

3 In the Name text box, type or paste a name for the new field.

4 In the Formula text box, enter the formula for this field.

   The formula can use Excel's built-in operators and functions, or change or combine one or more of the fields in the Fields list. To insert a field name in the formula quickly, double-click the name in the list. If you manually type a field name that contains spaces or special characters, enclose the name in single quotes ('Unit Price', for example).

5 Click OK.

   In the PivotTable Builder, Excel adds the calculated field to the fields list and the Values box, so that it appears in the pivot table (Figure 4.5). Excel sums the formula for every row.

   Removing a custom field from the Values box removes it from the pivot table, but it remains in the fields list for later use. To permanently delete a custom field, select it from the Name drop-down list in the Insert Calculated Field dialog box (shown above) and then click Delete.

Tip: To list all calculated fields in a new worksheet, choose PivotTable Analyze tab > Fields, Items, & Sets group > List Formulas.

Figure 4.4 Use the Insert Calculated Field dialog box to add a calculated field (formula) to a pivot table.

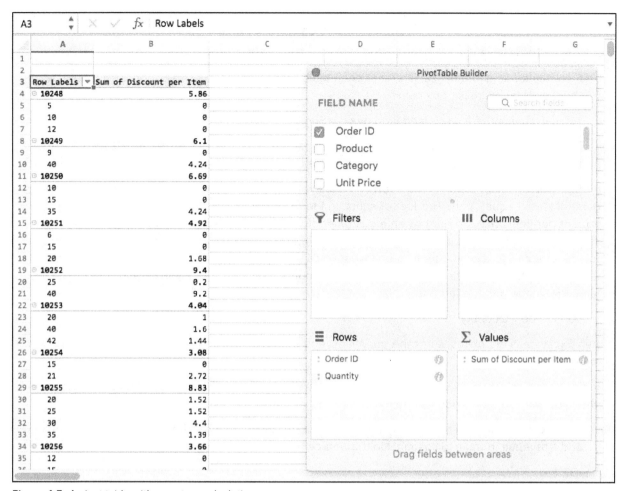

Figure 4.5 A pivot table with a custom calculation.

Troubleshooting Calculated Fields

Calculated fields have the following restrictions:

- A calculated-field formula can't refer to pivot-table grand totals or subtotals, nor can it refer to worksheet cells by address or by name.

- You can summarize a calculated field by only Sum.

- Because calculated-field formulas are always applied against the *sum* of the underlying data, Excel calculates data fields, subtotals, and grand totals before evaluating the calculated field.

In nontrivial formulas, the last restriction can cause unexpected results because the sum of products (generally) isn't equal to the product of sums. In the example above, the calculated field returns a 10 percent per-item price discount when a customer orders 20 or more units of a particular item, and no (zero) discount otherwise. In the resulting pivot table, the individual Quantity calculations are correct but the subtotals for each Order ID aren't what you'd expect (because Excel sums all an order's quantities *before* determining whether discounts apply). Another common trap: if you create a calculated field named Revenue with the formula:

='Unit Price' * Quantity

then Excel sums the prices, sums the quantities, and then multiplies the two sums—which is *not* what you want.

Sadly, there's no way to fix this problem, but there are a few (somewhat unsatisfying) workarounds for when you want sum-of-products and Excel is giving you product-of-sums:

- Add a column (field) to the underlying source data. In the sample workbook, for example, you can add a revenue formula to column J in the Source Data worksheet: type *Revenue* in cell J1, type:

=D2*E2

in cell J2 (Unit Price × Quantity), and then fill down (Ctrl+D) the J2 formula to the end of the data (cell J2156).

- Copy (Command+C) and paste values (Option+Command+V) from the pivot table to work with independently elsewhere in the workbook.

- Write formulas outside the pivot table. You might want to turn off the GETPIVOTDATA function when you write formulas that refer to a pivot table (PivotTable Analyze tab > PivotTable group > Options arrow > Generate GetPivotData toggle).

- Turn off grand totals and subtotals in the pivot table (Design tab) and then calculate your own totals outside the pivot table.

CHAPTER 5

Filtering Data

If a pivot table displays too much detail, you can **filter** (restrict) it to show only part of the source data. Excel offers several filters: report filters, slicers, and group filters.

Tip: If a pivot table's data source is a table (Insert tab > Tables group > Table), then any filters that you apply directly to the table have no effect on linked pivot tables. To filter data from a pivot table, you must use one of the methods described in this chapter.

Report Filters

Report filters let you filter out data so that a pivot table uses only rows of interest in the source data. Start with a pivot table with the settings:

Rows: Category
Columns: Ship City
Values: Quantity (summarized by Sum)
Filters: (empty)

Now, to create a summary for only specific countries, drag the field Ship Country to the Filters box. The report filter field appears just above the pivot table. (If you use more than one report filter, each appears in a separate row.) To set the filter, click the drop-down arrow ⬛ in the field box and then choose the countries that you want to display (Figure 5.1). To find an item, scroll the list or type the first few characters of its name in the search box. When you're done, click × (the red button). When a filter is applied, the field box button changes to 🔽.

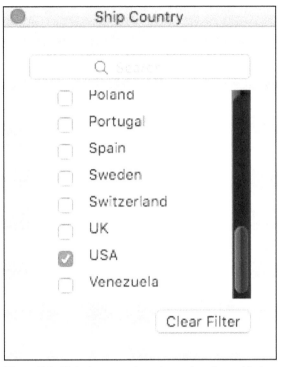

Figure 5.1 Click the arrow just above the pivot table to open the report filter drop-down list.

Tip: To control how report filter fields are arranged in rows and columns, choose PivotTable Analyze tab > PivotTable group > Options > Layout pane > "Report filter".

Excel uses checked items to create the pivot table, and ignores unchecked items (Figure 5.2). To quickly remove a report filter, choose the first item in the report filter list: "(Select All)" or click the Clear Filter button.

Tip: Any fields that you use for report filtering *can't* also be used for grouping (Chapter 3). If you filter by Ship Country, for example, you can't also group by Ship Country. This restriction doesn't apply to slicers and group filters.

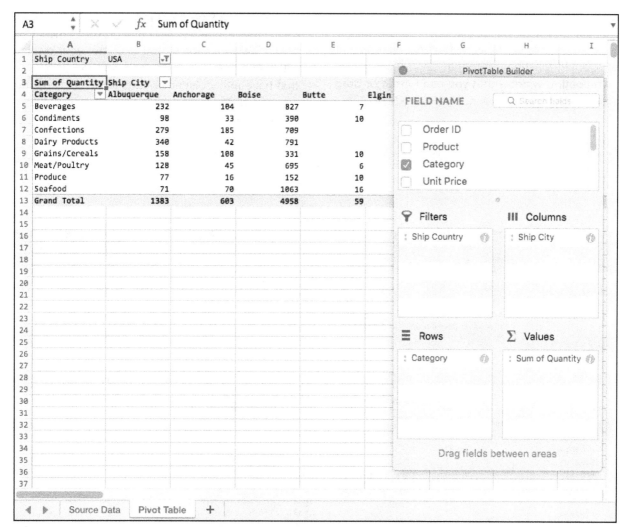

Figure 5.2 A pivot table with a report filter applied.

Slicers

Slicers offer about the same features as report filters, but in "dashboard" format. Each slicer has its own floating window that you can format or drag around the main Excel window (Figure 5.3).

By contrast with report filters, slicers offer fast one-click filtering, and can filter and group on the same field. However, slicers tend to clutter your display with floating windows and don't work well with fields that have many distinct values (which cause long scrolling distances). Also, slicers, like report filters, are less powerful than group filters.

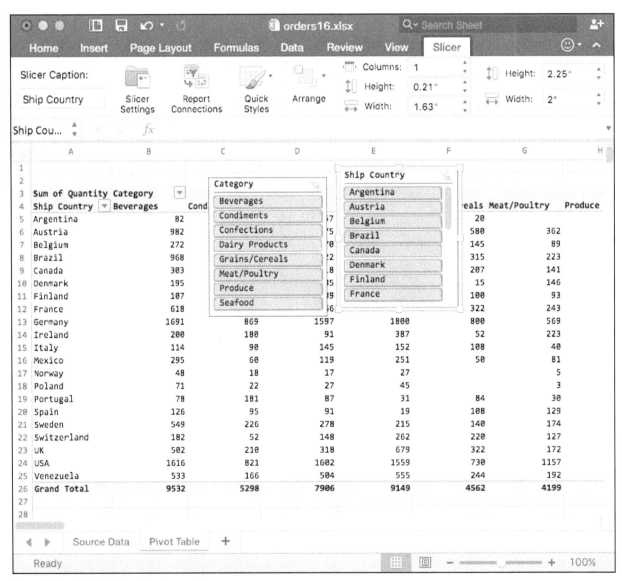

Figure 5.3 A pivot table with slicer windows.

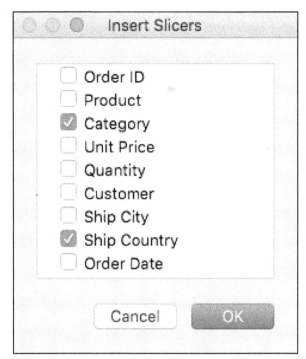

Figure 5.4 Use the Insert Slicers dialog box to select fields that you want to use for filtering.

To create a slicer:

1 Select any cell in the pivot table.

2 Choose PivotTable Analyze tab > Filter group > Insert Slicer.

   The Insert Slicers dialog box opens (Figure 5.4), listing all the fields in the pivot table (except custom fields, page 40).

3 Select the checkbox of each field that you want to use for filtering.

   Fields that have a small number of unique values make the best slicers because they fit well in a floating slicer window. Good choices: Category and Ship Country. Middling choices: Product and Customer. Poor choices: Unit Price and Order Date.

4 Click OK.

   Excel adds a separate floating window for each slicer.

5 Move or resize the floating slicer windows as desired.

   ▶ To move a slicer, point to a border (the pointer turns into a four-way arrow) and then drag.

   ▶ To resize a slicer, point to a corner or the middle of an edge (the pointer turns into a two-way arrow) and then drag.

   continues on next page

6 Use the slicer window to apply filtering (Figure 5.5). The slicer window lists all the unique values in a field, each value appearing as a separate button. The buttons of *visible* values are shaded. No filtering is in effect in a newly created slicer window, so every button is shaded.

▸ To filter on a single value, click its button.

▸ To filter on multiple values, hold down the Command key while you click each button. (To select a range of contiguous values, click the first button and then Shift-click the last button.)

▸ To clear filtering (show everything for the field), click the 🔽 button at the top of the slicer window.

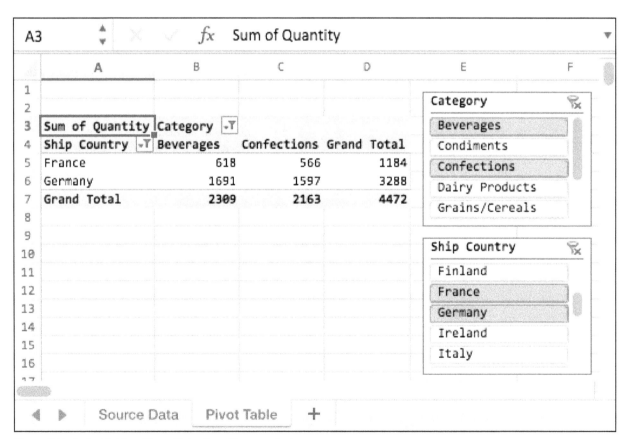

Figure 5.5 A pivot table with multiple slicer filters applied.

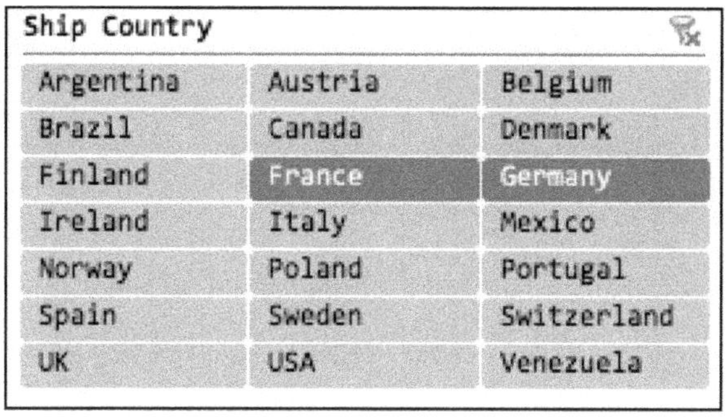

Ship Country		
Argentina	Austria	Belgium
Brazil	Canada	Denmark
Finland	France	Germany
Ireland	Italy	Mexico
Norway	Poland	Portugal
Spain	Sweden	Switzerland
UK	USA	Venezuela

Figure 5.6 A formatted slicer window.

7   (Optional) Format the slicer.

▶   To change the button colors, choose Slicer tab > Quick Styles.

▶   To expand or compact the slicer window, click the Slicer tab and then change the Columns, Height, and Width values. Figure 5.6 shows a three-column slicer window with custom button colors.

▶   To change the window title, choose Slicer tab > Slicer group > Slicer Caption box. To hide the window title, choose Slicer tab > Slicer group > Slicer Settings > clear "Display header".

▶   To sort a slicer's values, right click the slicer window and then choose a Sort command from the shortcut menu. Alternatively, choose Slicer tab > Slicer group > Slicer Settings > Item Sorting and Filtering.

▶   To remove a slicer, click it and then press Delete (or right-click it and then choose the Remove command from the shortcut menu).

Group Filters

Group filters—more powerful than report filters and slicers—let you filter fields that you're using to group a pivot table to:

- Show or hide specific items (like report filters, except that you can't create report filters for grouping fields).

- Create complex conditions that subset data. You can show or hide dates that fall in a specific time period, for example, or names that begin or end with a certain letter.

- Filter on multiple fields and configure them independently (Excel **additively** applies every filter at the same time).

The examples in this section use a pivot table with the settings (Figure 5.7):

Rows: Category, Product
Columns: Ship Country
Values: Quantity (summarized by Sum)
Filters: (empty)

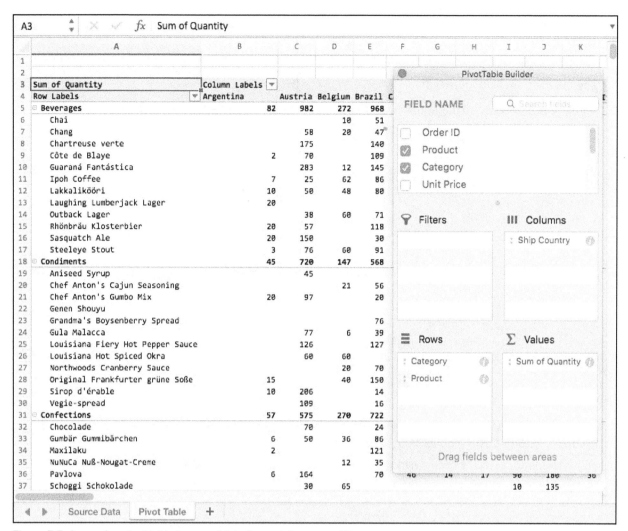

Figure 5.7 A complex pivot table is a candidate for applying group filters.

To create a group filter:

1 Click the drop-down arrow ▼ to the right of a Rows or Columns cell.

   The filter list opens (Figure 5.8).

2 If you're grouping on multiple fields, choose a field from the "Select field" drop-down list at top.

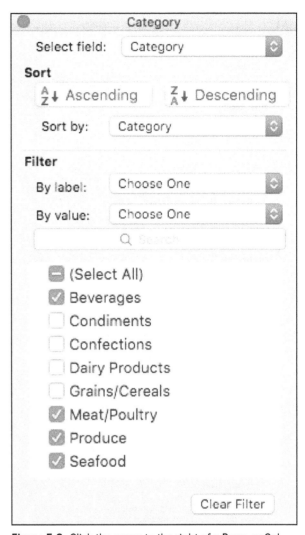

Figure 5.8 Click the arrow to the right of a Rows or Columns cell to open the group filter drop-down list.

Filtering Nested Fields

Label filters and value filters can get tricky when you work with nested fields (Chapter 2). The effect of the By Value > Less Than > 500 command, for example, differs depending on whether you apply it to the Product or Category field (recall that Product is nested within Category in this example). Applied to Product, the pivot table shows products that sold fewer than 500 units (as you'd expect). Applied to Category, only categories with sales fewer than 500 units across *all* their products appear. Because every category has sales greater than 500 units in the current example, the filter hides every category and shows an empty pivot table (which is correct logically but might not be what you'd expect).

Note that if you apply a filter to a Rows field (Category or Products, in this example), your Columns fields (Ship Country) have no effect. Likewise, row filters don't affect column filters.

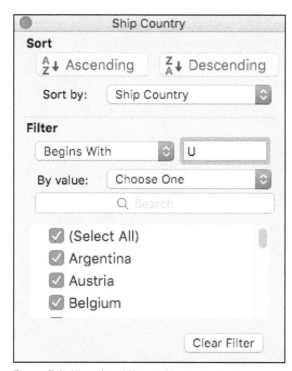

Figure 5.9 Use a label filter to filter by text values.

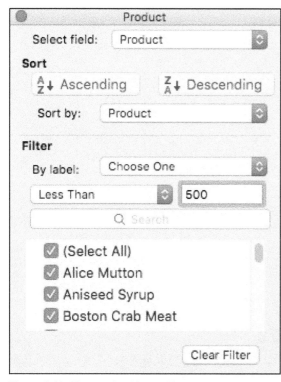

Figure 5.10 Use a value filter to filter by numeric values and ranges.

3 Set the desired options in the filter list and then click OK.

▶ To show or hide specific items, select or clear their checkboxes. To find an item, scroll the list or type the first few characters of its name in the search box.

▶ To show or hide items that contain specific text, begin or end with a certain letter, and so on, choose an option from the "By label" menu. To show only items that begin with "U", for example, choose Begins With and then type *U* in the text box that appears (Figure 5.9).

▶ To show or hide calculated values based on numerical criteria (less than, greater than, Top 10, and so on), choose an option from the "By value" menu. To show only items less than 500, for example, choose Less Than and then type *500* in the text box that appears (Figure 5.10).

▶ To sort items, click Ascending or Descending. To use a custom sort order, choose PivotTable Analyze tab > PivotTable group > Options > Layout pane > Sort.

▶ To remove a filter (show everything for the field), click the Clear Filter button. If you have multiple filters, you must remove each one separately. To remove them all at once (and show all data), choose PivotTable Analyze tab > Actions group > Clear > Clear Filters.

Tip: When a filter is applied, the button to the right of the Rows or Columns cell changes to ⏷.

---

4 To filter by other grouping fields, repeat the preceding steps for each row label or column label.

CHAPTER 6

Tricks with Pivot Tables

Excel's arsenal of pivot-table features offers a few nonobvious ways to solve common problems.

Creating a Frequency Tabulation

You can use a pivot table to quickly create a frequency tabulation for a single column of data. In the sample workbook, for example, switch to the Source Data worksheet, select the Ship Country column (click the H column heading), choose Insert tab > Tables group > PivotTable, and then create the pivot table. In the PivotTable Builder, drag the Ship Country field into the Rows box and then drag it again into the Values box. The resulting pivot table tallies the number of times that each country appears in the column (Figure 6.1). You can group, filter, and chart this tabulation as you would any pivot table. See also "Grouping by Numbers" on page 34.

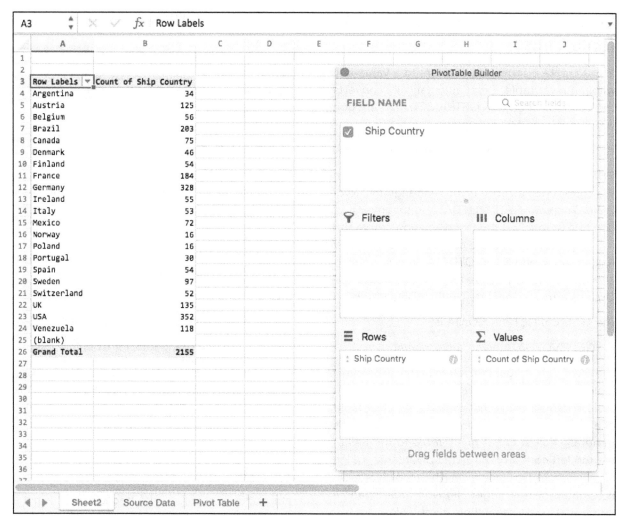

Figure 6.1 A pivot table showing a frequency tabulation.

Controlling References to Pivot Table Cells

If you create a formula that refers to a value cell within a pivot table, Excel automatically converts the cell reference to a GETPIVOTDATA function with arguments. For example:

    =GETPIVOTDATA(A3, "Argentina Beverages")

GETPIVOTDATA ensures that formulas still return the correct results even if you rearrange the pivot table. To avoid GETPIVOTDATA autoconversion, don't point to (click) the cell when you create the formula; instead, type the cell reference manually. To turn on or off GETPIVOTDATA autoconversion, choose PivotTable Analyze tab > PivotTable group > Options arrow > Generate GetPivotData toggle.

The syntax of GETPIVOTDATA is:

    GETPIVOTDATA(*pivot_table*, *name*)

The *pivot_table* argument refers to the target pivot table and can be a cell or range of cells in the pivot table, a named range that contains the pivot table, or a label stored in a cell above the pivot table. It's generally safest to set *pivot_table* to the cell at the top left corner of the target pivot table, which stays anchored in place even when the pivot table is updated or rearranged. If *pivot_table* spans a range that contains multiple pivot tables (not recommended), then GETPIVOTDATA retrieves a value from whichever pivot table was created most recently in that range.

The *name* argument is a quote-enclosed string that describes the cell in *pivot_table* that contains the value to return, provided that value is visible in *pivot_table*.

Consider a pivot table with the settings (Figure 6.2):

Rows: Category
Columns: Ship Country
Values: Quantity (summarized by Sum)
Filters: (empty)

The formula:

    =GETPIVOTDATA(A3, "Argentina Beverages")

returns 82, and:

    =GETPIVOTDATA(A3, "Condiments Austria")

returns 720.

The formula:

    =GETPIVOTDATA(A3, "Argentina")

returns 339 (the grand total for Argentina), and:

    =GETPIVOTDATA(A3, "Condiments")

returns 5298 (the grand total for Condiments).

Rearranging the pivot table doesn't affect the results; the preceding formulas would still return the same values if you dragged Category to Columns or dragged Ship Country to Rows.

The formula:

    =GETPIVOTDATA(A3, "Argentina Fruit")

returns the error value #N/A because Fruit is not a valid Category value.

If you filter the pivot table (Chapter 5) to hide Argentina or Beverages, then the formula:

    =GETPIVOTDATA(A3, "Argentina Beverages")

returns the error value #REF!.

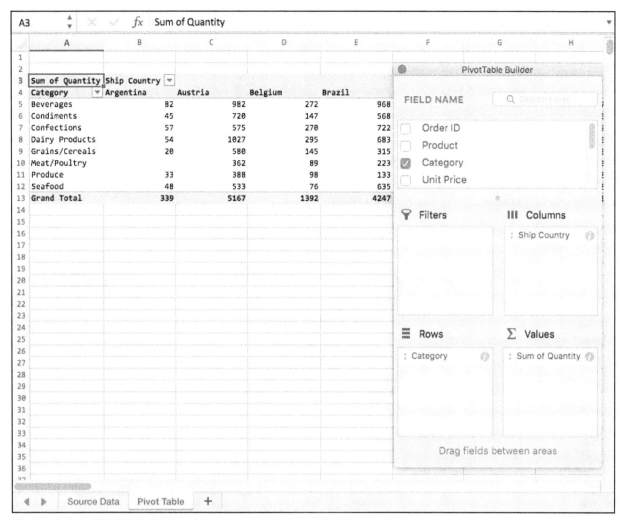

Figure 6.2 The GETPIVOTDATA formulas in this section refer to this pivot table.

Replicating a Pivot Table for Report Filter Items

You can set up a pivot table and then replicate it for every distinct value of a report filter (page 44). This feature isn't popular because it generates multiple pivot tables when a single nested and filtered pivot table should suffice for most purposes. It may be useful for generating separate tables or charts to paste in different slides in a presentation.

Consider a pivot table with the settings (Figure 6.3):

Rows: Category
Columns: (empty)
Values: Quantity (summarized by Sum)
Filters: Ship Country

Choose PivotTable Analyze tab > PivotTable group > Options arrow > Show Report Filter Pages. In the Show Pages dialog box that opens, select Ship Country and then click OK. Excel replicates the pivot table for every country, creating a worksheet for each new pivot table (inspect the worksheet tabs at the bottom of the Excel window) (Figure 6.4).

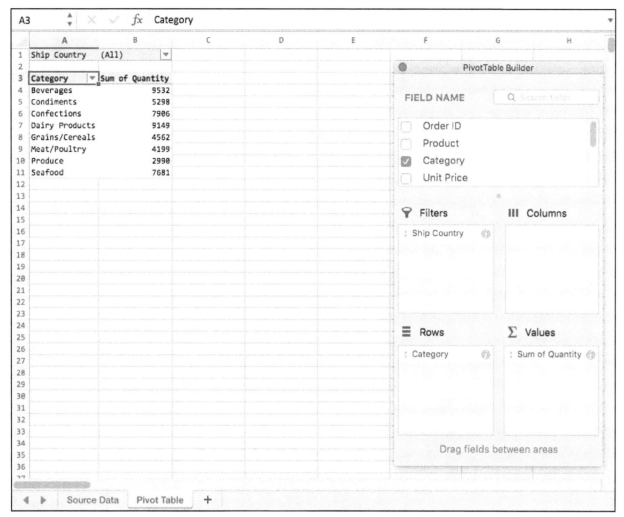

Figure 6.3 A pivot table to be replicated by Ship Country.

Figure 6.4 Worksheet tabs for replicated pivot tables.

Index